The KID'S Progressive Alef~Bet

2

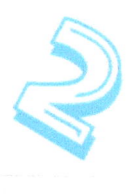

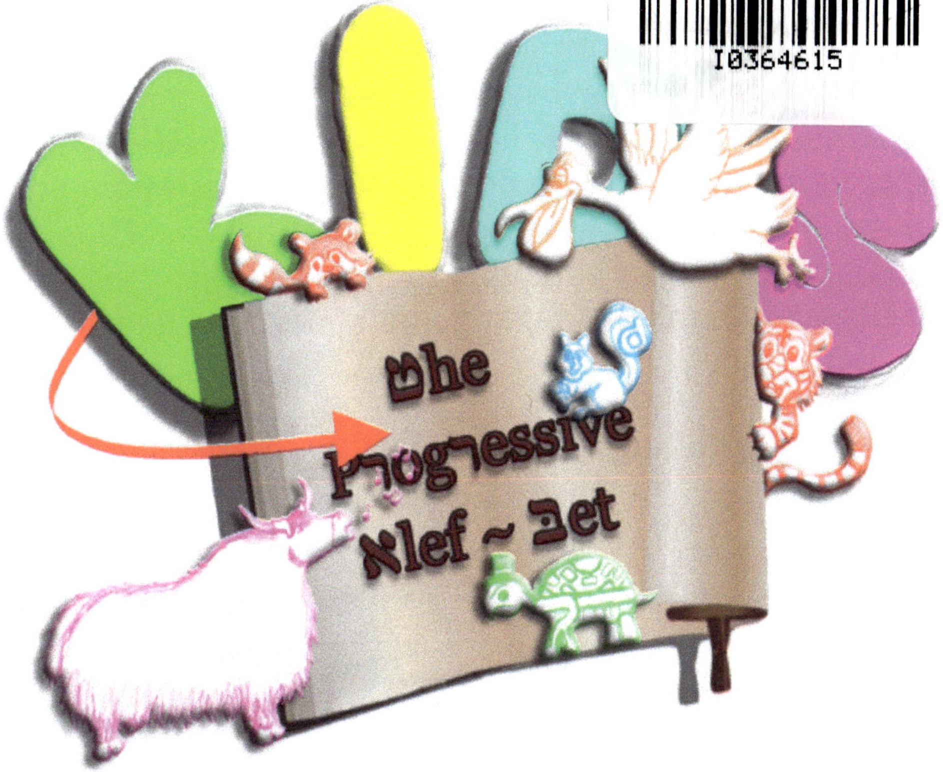

BOOK TWO:
THE VOWELS

written by Ahava Lilburn
illustrated by Kelsey Lilburn

A note to the reader:

The Hebrew vowels are small markings that can be found in specific locations around the letters. A vowel is usually pronounced **after** the letter it is associated with.

Memorizing the name of the vowels is not as important as being able to connect the sound the vowel makes with the image of the vowel.

Each of the vowels in this book have been associated with a specific color to help with the learning process. Most of the colors are pretty common, however, the final vowel (Sheva) can be associated with Pumpkin Orange. This is because the Sheva /Sh'va/ can either be silent or sound like the "u" in "pumpkin".

A simplified way to remember if the Sheva is silent or makes a sound: if it begins a word or syllable then it makes a sound if it is at the close of a word or syllable then it is silent. So, the Sheva announces itself as it enters and is silent as it leaves!

produced by Minister 2 Others

ISBN 978-1-7324223-6-0

copyright 2018 Minister 2 Others

Minister2others.com

Hebrew Vowels are not so complicated
Match the colors that make their sound
Note how the vowel is situated
And you'll soon know the Hebrew Vowels!

ָ	/ah/	*below* ִ	/ēe/
ַ	/ah/	יִ	/ēe/
הָ	/ah/	יָ	/ī/
ֱ	/eh/	יַ	/ī/
ֶ	/eh/	*above and left* ֹ	/ō/
ֵ	/ay/	וֹ	/ō/
יֵ	/ay/	ֻ	/ū/
יֱ	/ay/	וּ	/ū/
		ְ	silent / slur

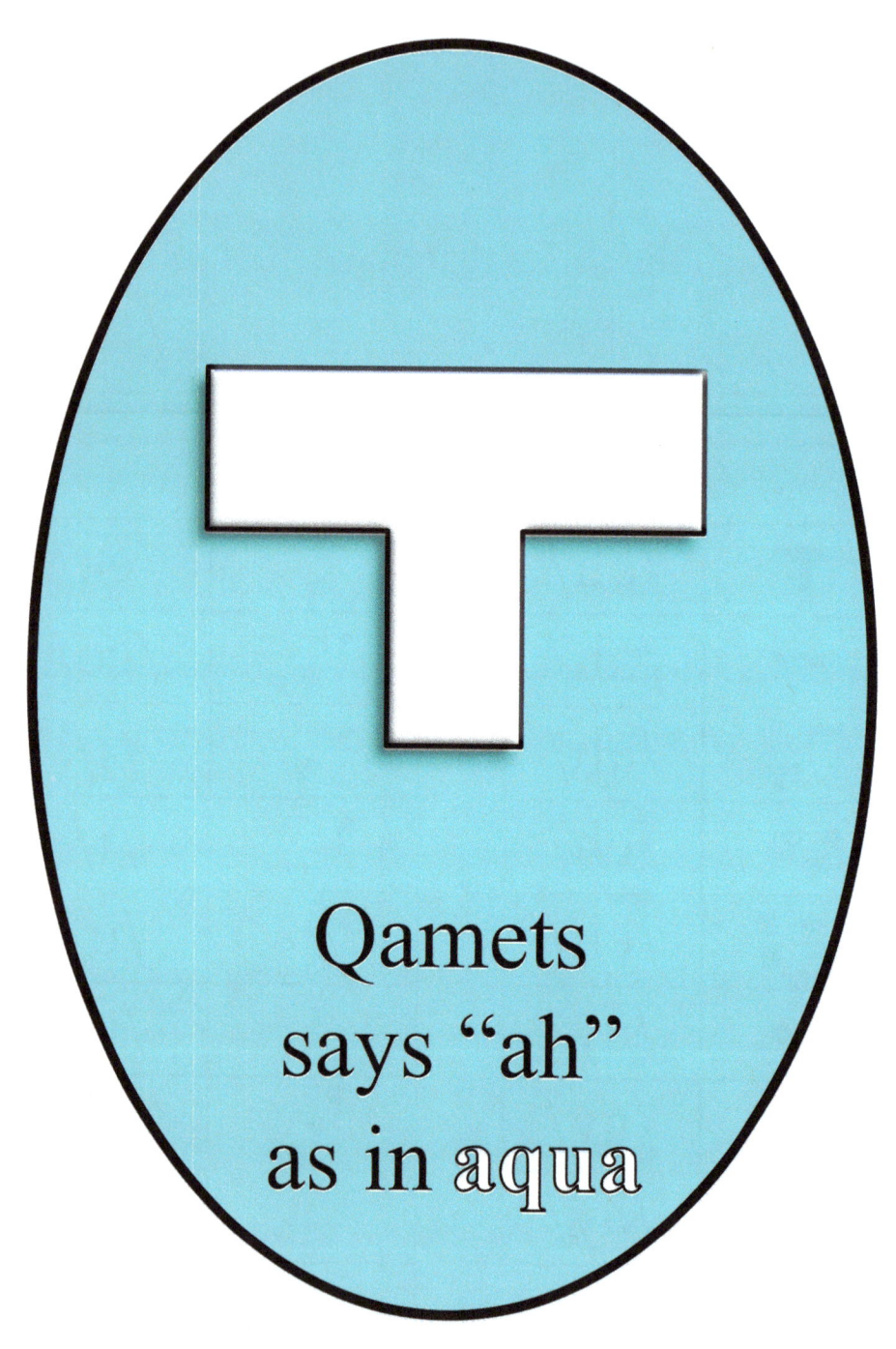

This vowel is located under a letter.

אַn a smאַll table
just down the הַll,
there is a לַrge vase
with flowers and עַll.

Can you spot this vowel in the picture?

*(On a small table just down the hall,
there is a large vase with flowers and all.)*

This vowel is located under a letter.

A seagull dרְssed
a little נֶst
where three small אֶggs
could be at רֶst.

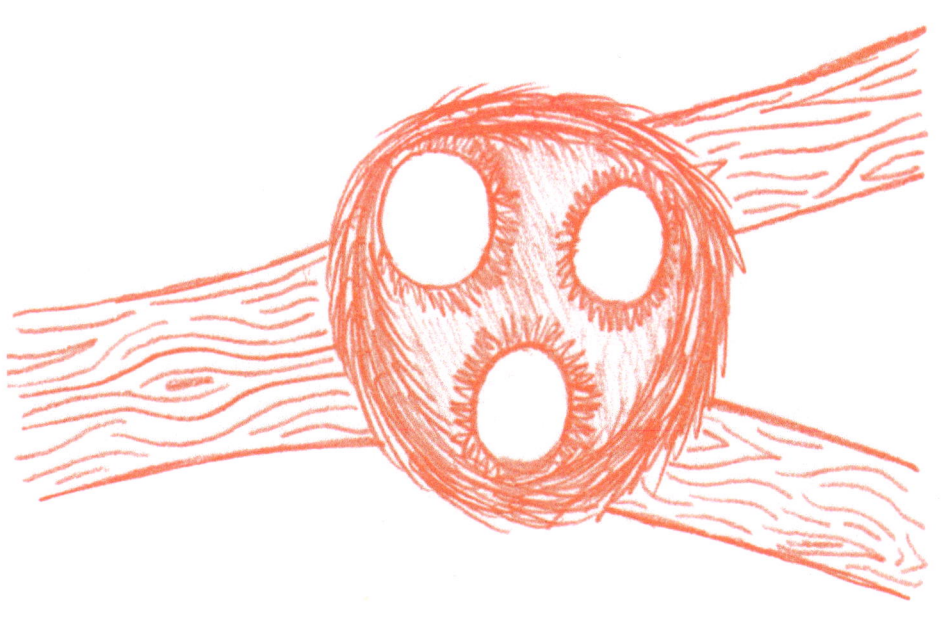

Can you spot this vowel in the picture?

*(A seagull dressed a little nest
where three small eggs could be at rest.)*

This vowel is located under a letter.

כֵּcey got a bicycle,
it was bent and gרֵ
She stרֵtened it and פֵּnted it,
then sתֵed on it all דֵ

Can you spot this vowel in the picture?

*(Kacey got a bicycle, it was bent and gray.
She straightened it and painted it,
then stayed on it all day!)*

This vowel is located under a letter.

ךְ gets her hoנַ
from a בּ
who לְves it
way up in a tרְ

Can you spot this vowel in the picture?

*(Dee gets her honey from a bee
who leaves it way up in a tree.)*

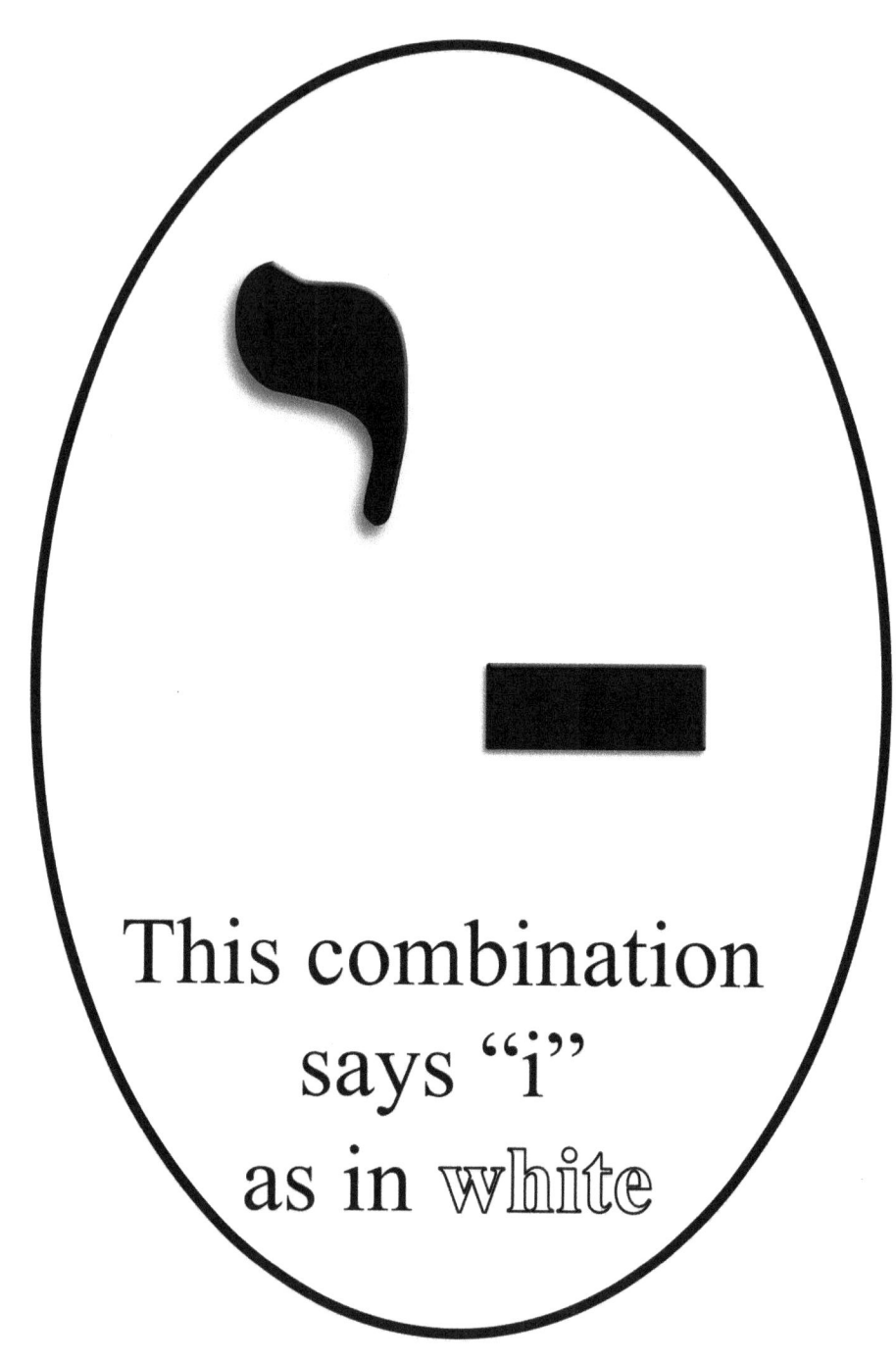

This is a combination vowel called a diphthong. This is made with a Patach under a letter, directly followed by the letter Yod.

Wh אַ does a שִׁ wink,
מִי one עַיּ closed,
make פִּve little wrinkles
on the סִde of מִי nose?

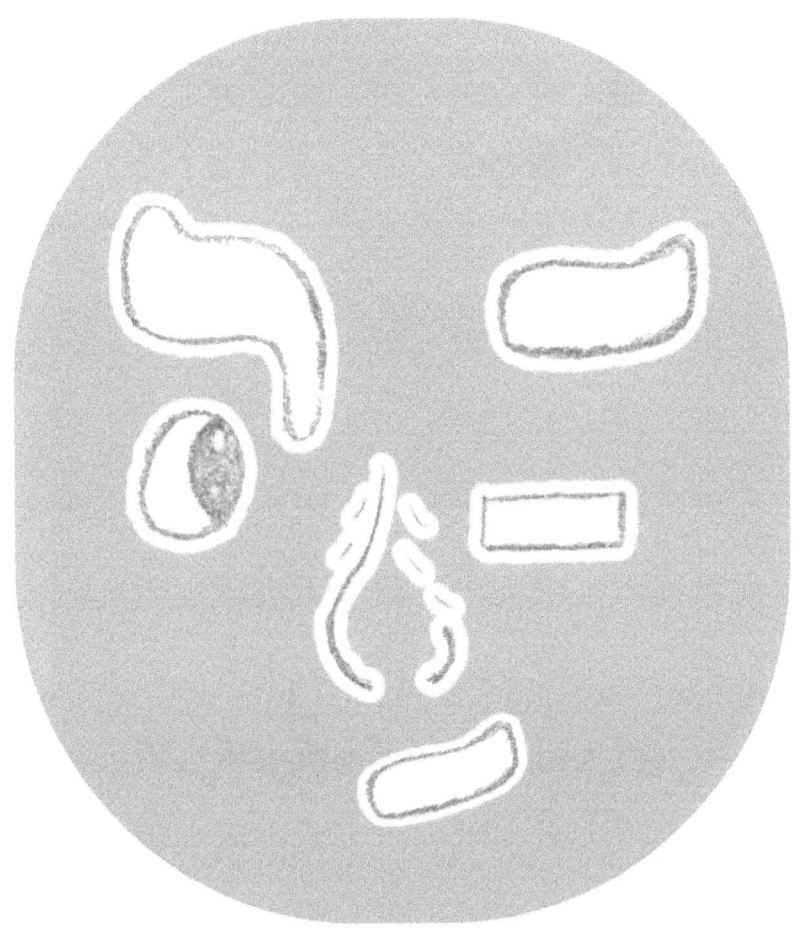

Can you spot this vowel in the picture?

*(Why does a shy wink, my one eye closed,
make five little wrinkles on the side of my nose?)*

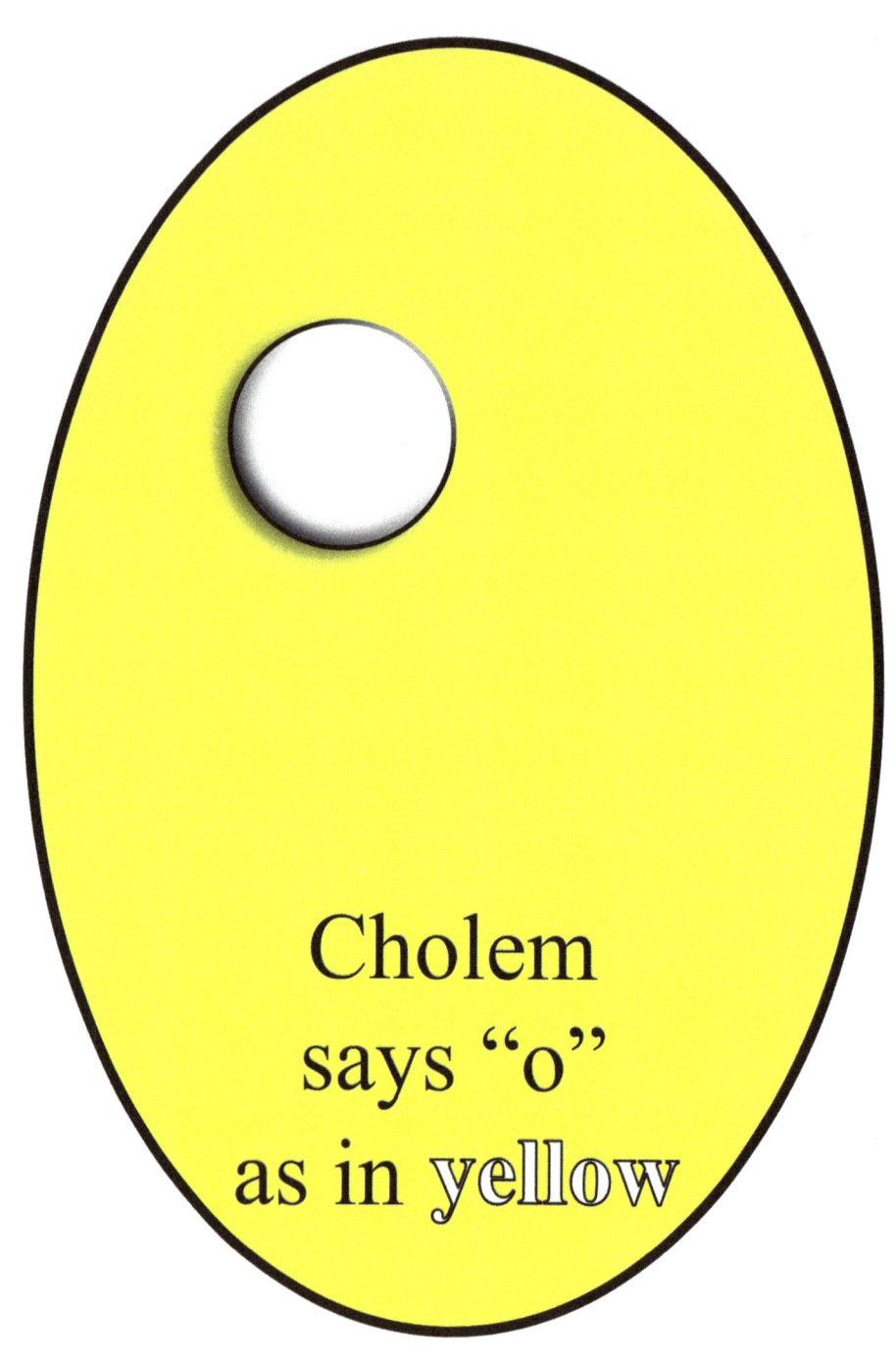

Cholem says "o" as in yellow

This vowel is located above and to the left of a letter.

My sנman lost
his carrot נse.
He got סקld,
he alנst fרze!

Can you spot this vowel in the picture?

*(My snowman lost his carrot nose.
He got so cold, he almost froze!)*

This vowel is located under a letter.

I heard a נָ song,
דְּ Bee דְּ דְּ
I'll cרוּn this סְthing תֵּne
for יָ

Can you spot this vowel in the picture?

*(I heard a new song - Doo Bee Doo Doo
I'll croon this soothing tune for you!)*

This vowel is located under a letter.

בּb has a בֶּx
that holds אַll his things --
לַts of cool רַcks
and a big בַּll of string.

Can you spot this vowel in the picture?

*(Bob has a box that holds all his things --
lots of cool rocks and a big ball of string.)*

This vowel is located under a letter.

A סֶcond seagull
came to cרֶst,
סֶtting two more ֶעggs
in the first bird's נst.

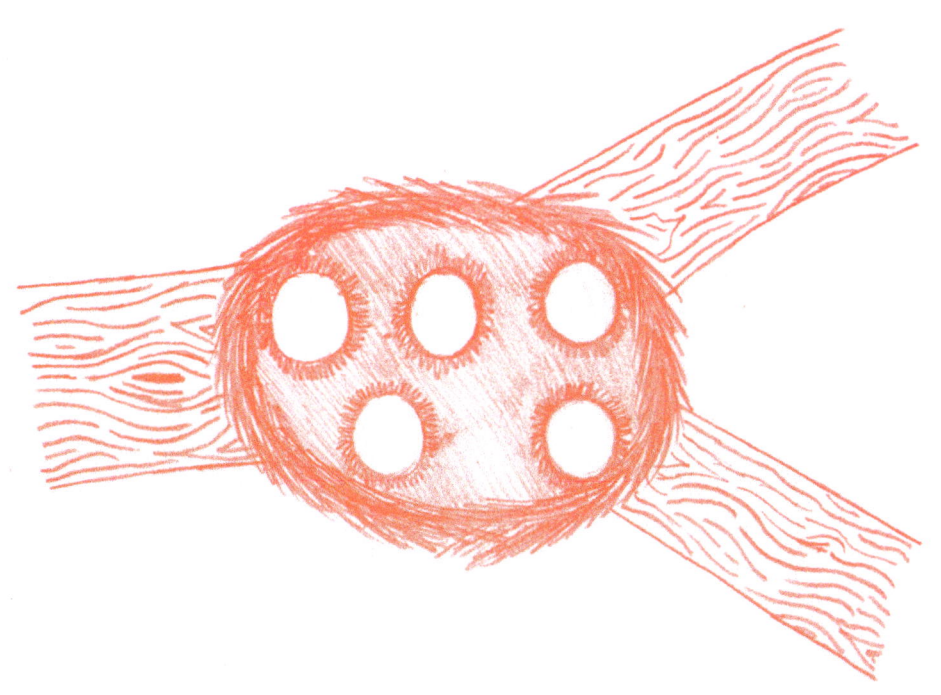

Can you spot this vowel in the picture?

*(A second seagull came to crest,
setting two more eggs in the first bird's nest.)*

This vowel has a Tsere under a letter,
directly followed by the letter Yod.

רֵי took his wagon
outside to pלֵי
A stרֵי cat לֵd down
right in his wאֵי

Can you spot this vowel in the picture?

*(Ray took his wagon outside to play.
A stray cat laid down right in his way!)*

This vowel has a Chireq under a letter, directly followed by the letter Yod.

לִי threw a ball
at Sal and מִי
that's why שִׁי threw it back,
you שִׂי

Can you spot this vowel in the picture?

*(Lee threw a ball at Sal and me,
that's why she threw it back, you see!)*

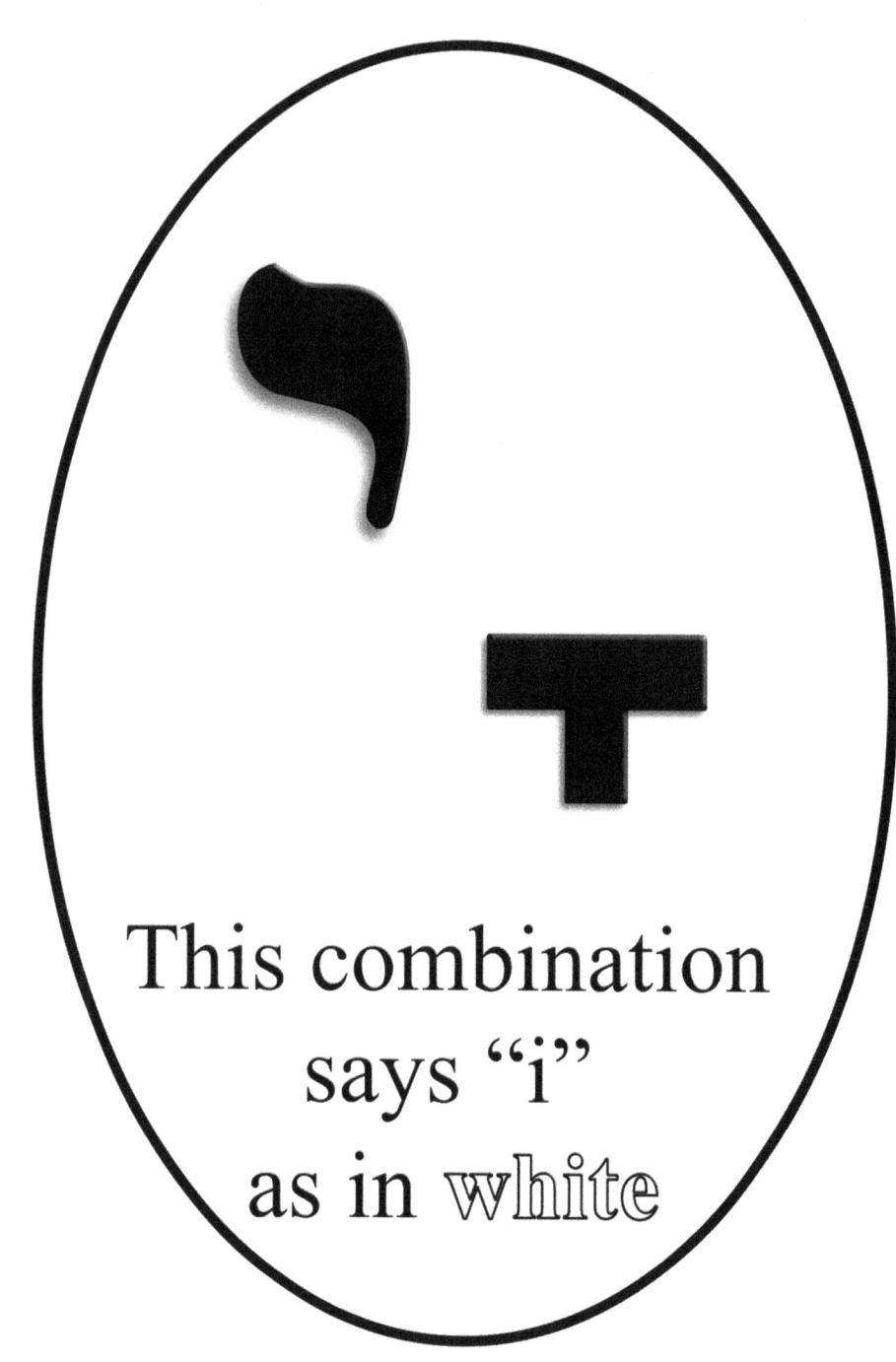

This is a combination vowel called a diphthong. This is made with a Qamets under a letter, directly followed by the letter Yod.

Above the wאָre,
כָּי הָי in the sי
מָי great big קִּte
goes fבִּילָing

Can you spot this vowel in the picture?

*(Above the wire, high in the sky,
my great big kite goes flying by.)*

This vowel is located to the left of a letter.

מוֹs וֹהle net
had הוֹles נוּ doubt!
He'd thרוֹr cרוֹs in,
cרוֹs would גוֹ out!

Can you spot this vowel in the picture?

*(Mo's whole net had holes, no doubt!
He'd throw crows in, crows would go out!)*

This vowel is located to the left of a letter.

יוּ see that fרוּt.
It לוּks real fine!
It's גוּd and ripe!
This פוּd's all mine!

Can you spot this vowel in the picture?

*(You see that fruit - it looks real fine!
It's good and ripe - this food's all mine!)*

This vowel has a Qamets under a letter, directly followed by the letter Hey.

Outside the little דָהghouse,
a springler פָּה pטָה ps up.
It wאָhters the ground around it,
soaking הall and my sמַהll pup!

Can you spot this vowel in the picture?

*(Outside the little doghouse, a springler top pops up.
It waters the ground around it,
soaking all and my small pup!)*

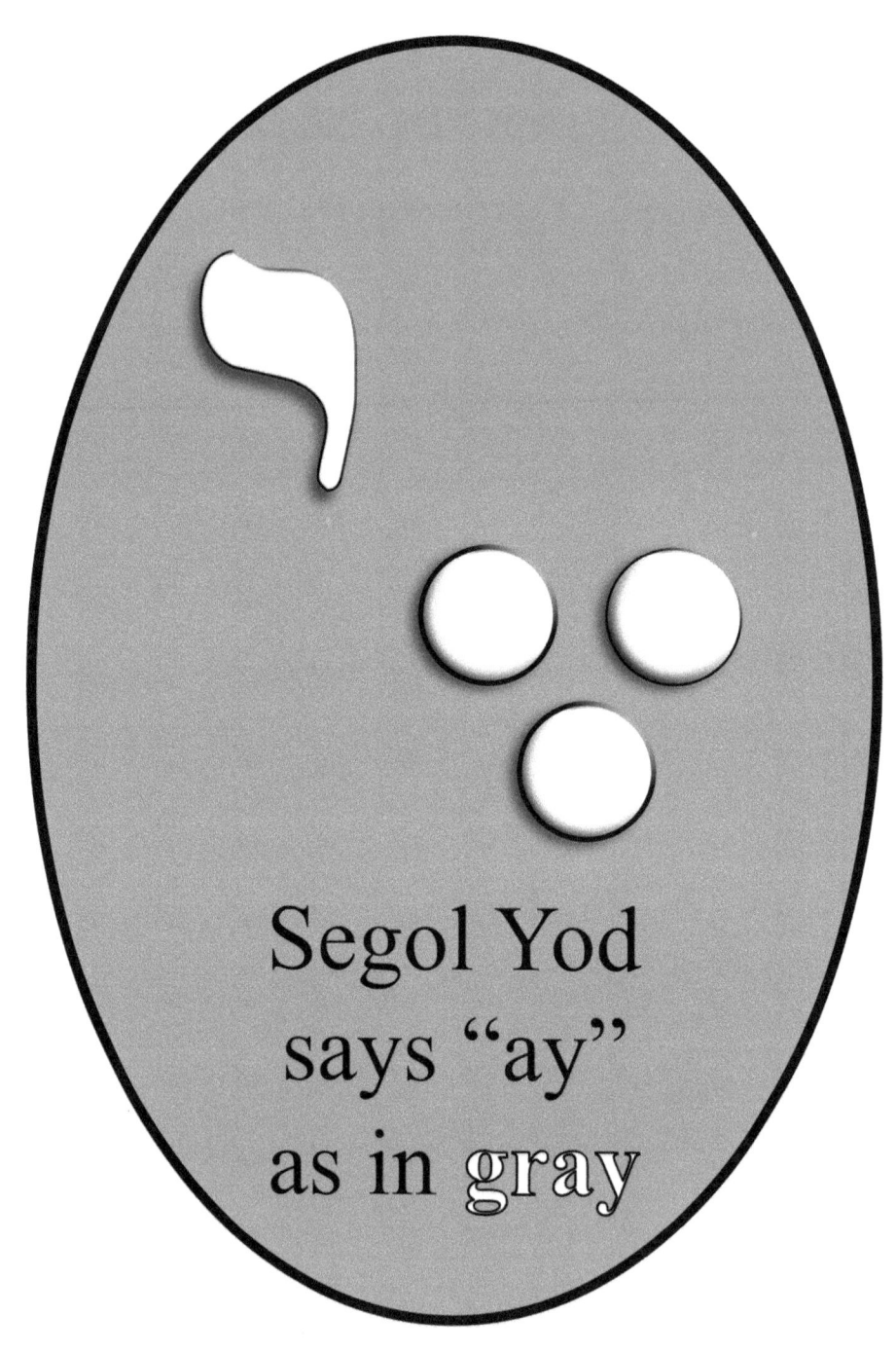

This vowel has a Segol under a letter, directly followed by the letter Yod.

My gרַֽי pupply
likes to pלַֽי
He tilts his פֶּֽce
in funny wעֶֽs!

Can you spot this vowel in the picture?

*(My gray pupply likes to play.
He tilts his face in funny ways!)*

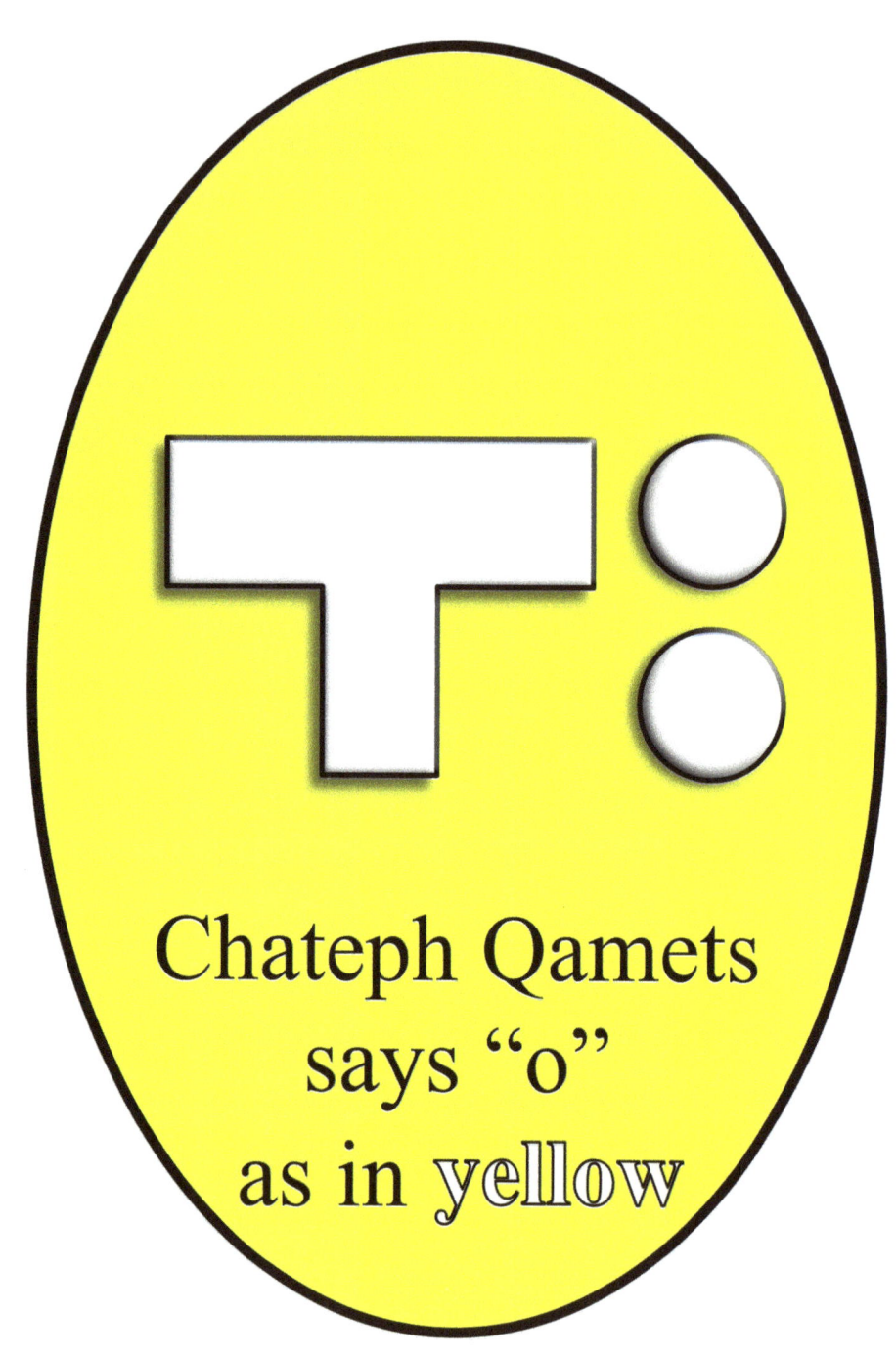

This vowel is located under a letter.

Two רֶlls upon the table
רֶll sלֶly to the fלֶr
אַh נֶ we cannot catch them!
I really הֶpe there's מֶre!"

Can you spot this vowel in the picture?

*(Two rolls upon the table fall slowly to the floor
Oh no, we cannot catch them!
I really hope there's more!)*

This vowel is located under a letter.

Liכְּ a stoפְּlighתְ
with only two קְlors,
שְׁva stops syלְלְbles
uנְlike the others!

Can you spot this vowel in the picture?

*(Like a stoplight with only two colors,
Sheva stops syllables - unlike the others!)*

www.ingramcontent.com/pod-product-compliance
Lightning Source LLC
Chambersburg PA
CBHW061235070526
44584CB00030B/4135